salmonpoetry

Diverse Voices from Ireland and the World

OTHER POETRY BY MARK GRANIER

Ghostlight: New & Selected Poems (Salmon, 2017)

Haunt (Salmon, 2015)

Fade Street (Salt, 2010)

The Sky Road (Salmon, 2007)

Airborne (Salmon, 2001)

Everything You Always Wanted To Know

Mark Granier

Published in 2025 by
Salmon Poetry
Cliffs of Moher, County Clare, Ireland
Website: www.salmonpoetry.com
Email: info@salmonpoetry.com

Copyright © Mark Granier, 2025

ISBN 978-1-915022-81-3

All rights reserved. No part of this publication may be reproduced or transmitted in any form or by any means, electronic or mechanical, including photography, recording, or any information storage or retrieval system, without permission in writing from the publisher. The book is sold subject to the condition that it shall not, by way of trade or otherwise, be lent, resold or otherwise circulated without the publisher's prior consent in any form of binding or cover other than that in which it is published and without a similar condition, including this condition, being imposed on the subsequent purchaser.

Cover Photography: Mark Granier
Design & Typesetting: Siobhán Hutson Jeanotte

Printed in Ireland by Sprint Print

Salmon Poetry gratefully acknowledges the support of
The Arts Council / An Chomhairle Ealaíon

For my friends

After A Painting By Qin Tianzhu

*The ink-blot bird — composed
of a handful
of feathery strokes —*

*seems so slight
that if it flitted off
it would not leave one*

*splayed, spidery print
on the white
page, the snow,*

*let alone lift
a corner of this
blankness to which*

it is directly opposed.

Contents

To The Pavement	13
Anyway	14
Brevities	15
Ashen	16
Eyes	18
Listening to Bray	19
Grass	21
Dublin, 5.32 p.m., May 17, 1974	22
Civil	23
Swathe	24
Sirens	25
Night Run, Mount Merrion	26
Roundstone	27
A Brief History Of Snowflakes	28
Collectors' Items	29
Beds	30
Nativity	31
Marvellous	32
'There Is No Loitering Permitted Till 7 a.m.'	34
Newts	35
Torremolinos, 1972	36
Pinball Wizard	38
'Alright, Full Auto'	39
Gastarbeiter	40
Customs	41
Wild Garlic	42
The Air, The Aether	43
From The East	44
In The Name Of	45
Just Now	46
Song Between Seasons	47
Westport, Late August	48

Two Street Portraits	49
Accosted	50
Workshop	51
On Difficulty	52
Footnotes For Ovid	53
Latinate	55
From The Irish: Three Triads And Two Fragments	56
Pangur Dubh	57
Silk	58
Pub	60
Crossing Hungerford Bridge	61
Three Towers	62
The Verdict On Chagall	64
Deansgrange Similes	65
Two Endings	66
Bodily	68
Colonoscopy	69
Post Op	70
Mixture	71
Mark	72
Crown Shyness	74
Understory	75
Everything You Always Wanted To Know	76
The Themes	77
20-1-18	78
The End, Etc.	79
Checkout	80
Ah, Jesus	81
Road	82
Notes	84
Acknowledgements	86
About the author	88

To The Pavement

Great welcome mat
bled on, pissed on, dressed up
in the rain-slicked night's lurid
dabble of lights, or midsummer's
long-legged shadow-puppetry —
treadmill, hard mattress,
you take the daily weight of us
and our absence: dawn cities
littered with gulls, blue light
leaking like Revelation, the slow
mechanised whine of road cleaners
gathering in the sheaves —

Anyway,

it is the same walk
with the same friends, cousins,
our conversation a circuit

of concerns — new aches, old
ribbing, politics — the pattern
so worn we can trace it

with a guffaw, a full-bellied sigh
that returns us to marvel at
how easily we become what

we are, impossibly in our sixties,
putting on our new
old-men clothes with only

marginally more difficulty;
who feel, creaking beside us,
the companionship of that

baffling contraption, the past,
and how aimless
is the approach of the great

nothing: footfalls, the wheel
vanishing under the wheel
with these tensile

silences that build
in the gaps between words,
never quite closing when

one of us takes up the thread
to let the frayed end
have its say, murmuring

our old refrain: *Anyway*

Brevities

...a brief crack of light between two eternities of darkness.
— Vladimir Nabokov

TIME

It's odder than we used to think
on our heavenly body
wearing its wristwatch of seasons.

OPTICAL CLOCK

Late again, always late
despite your head
running faster than your feet.

LIFT

Going up? Down? What floor
on this floorless shaft through the days,
this bubble of air?

EVERYTHING

worth saying
has been said, says the rain
saying it again.

A TIME

1999, Crete, that pop song
wafted along an avenue of cicadas
replaying like Once upon

ENTROPY

Heat death of the universe, don't worry,
I'm already ahead of you,
I'll turn out the light.

Ashen

I scoop a fistful
of a man I'd spoken to
almost exactly a year ago:

my wife's stepfather — a gentle
geologist who liked to talk
about things like this —

from whom I inherited a pair
of black fingerless gloves
and a tall stack

of *New Scientist* journals
it would take
what's left of my life to read;

who specified that his body
be donated to medicine,
not knowing they

would have enough bodies
to work with; so
his backup wish, to be

lightened to this
grittiness, a creamy grey
with brighter grains

scattered by family and friends
in the woods where
he walked every day (a footfall

quietly removed). I let
trickle another handful,
like sand on a beach, or some

substance that does not
slow the passage of thought —
glancing at my palm, chalky

against dark grass and ferns,
as if I'd swiped it across
a classroom blackboard

littered with those
smoky numbers and letters
that put me to sleep —

Eyes

Images, images... We have always praised
that part of our flesh that sees —
baby-blue, sparkling, sultry, clear, or eyes

as unremarkable as mine,
a murky, greenish brown. I can see now
the gold eyes of the black cat

she adopted in '82, but not
hers: the first woman I lived with.
It's her lovely open face I won't forget.

The expressionist mask in which our glance is set
is what we are often speaking of when
we say that someone's eyes shine,

though it might be hands that define
a nimble and knowledgeable warmth. Close
your eyes. No need to probe

this dark, to find a membrane
for a soul to lean out and tell us what
we know we're at, trailing through each other like rain.

Listening To Bray

I am listening to Istanbul with my eyes closed
— Orhan Veli Kanik

I am listening to Bray with my eyes half-closed,
attempting to tune in
to this town we've settled in: the faint burr
of passing voices, racket of sparrows
in the moss-choked gutter, overscored
by a heavy engine, the bin truck
beeping as it backs up —

I am listening to the drunk I heard
while reading in bed the first night
we moved in: a slurred roar:
Don't you fucking walk away from me!

I am listening to the thunder of skateboards
on the newly paved area around
the touched-up Victorian bandstand:
a remnant from the old postcards
in which Bray Head has yet to be crowned
with its concrete cross, and the mile-long prom brims
with bowler hats, boaters, parasols,
warm-blooded chatter among the perpetual
blustery waves and gulls —

I am listening to what occupies, today,
the hulk of the old BRAY HEAD HOTEL
(that became, for a while, B AY HEAD,
till more letters fell.) No guests there now
to interrupt the sea's breathing or be rattled awake
by a train on the nearby track —

I am listening to the weave of sirens
threading the clogged main street, its traffic
idling downhill from the town hall

to the humpbacked bridge over the ruddy-brown
Dargle: smacking of wings as four swans
race for lift-off, laughter
followed by coughing from the bevy of afternoon drinkers
who gather every day at the same bench
to knock back a few cans, take in the slack,
holding court in the presence of water
that is always loitering and always elsewhere —

Grass
— Bray Head, 2020

I don't think I've ever seen grass

this luxuriant, a seedy, waist-high crop
cresting over, deepening the thin trodden paths,
(two children bright as crayons, walking a dog
through the frothy, sibilant sea).
                                  Rampant wild grass —
with a light breeze searching for a parting —
that keeps the whole slope weaving and unweaving.

Bend closer, and each shivering tip rises,
tapestry-bright, distinct as a headdress
or a working quill, as if the field were breathlessly
inscribing its own epic.
                      What are you —

Tufted Hair? Canary? Lyme? Meadow Fescue?
Crested Dog's-Tail? Meadow Cat's-Tail? Common Bent?

I must now add to my ignorance of birdcalls
this illegible grass, flattened here and there with forms
where families had picnicked or lovers rolled —

Bespoke grass, tailor-made for a doze,
grass to lose a million needles in
or find them. Grass working its shuttle loom.
Grass to make wishes on. Grass with no design
other than to be grass

feathering its own nest. Grass like us.

Dublin, 5.32pm, May 17, 1974

for Patrick Mac Allister

You're crossing from Mount Street to Merrion Square

when the third one goes off, just ahead, near
Greene's Bookshop — Blitzed glass

(from windows that had reflected an overcast
Friday evening sky) crunch underfoot

as you find yourself among the dazed or cut
spilling from shops and offices.

And the bodies? You don't stop
to look, but keep on as if guided through

what the evening has been displaced to
(by the ones who are all business.) Still clear

in your distracted head, after fifty years.
I said 'Imagine if you'd got there a moment earlier...'

And you: 'Believe it or not, I had never
thought of that...'

A coordinate on the unsmoothed, breathing map,
you cross the city, climb

the creaky stairs to your Biology grind
in a room down by the quays, where you try

to concentrate while sirens swarm around you —
the country of the living, still so wide,

its borders hold you easily, mid-stride —

Civil

One of my grandfather's brothers, Charlie,
approached my aunt's husband-to-be
at their engagement party,

and said to Pat, this fiancé
Charlie had never met — moreover,
said with a smile, as if it were a joke

worth sharing — 'We shot your uncle.'

Swathe

Some still remember the Iliad
of insects, the soft flick
of mayflies — bodies too small
to be swatted — hitting the glass,
our summery slipstream dense
with flight paths ending in smears
of sticky ichor, the flailing
of impotent wipers: air
a rippling long acre
ferrying wave after wave,
assailing us with the rumour
of something advancing: a margin
clearing and closing in.

Sirens

for Duncan

At intervals, in our edgy little town,
that shrill note rises and falls

and our collie answers it. He stands
in the back yard, lifts his wolfy muzzle

and adds something desolate and beautiful —
a lament, a full-throated dirge —

to the Great Book of Warnings and Wounds:
sheep torn from the flock,

a human slipped from the pack.
Only a dog knows how to sing

to a siren. Here he comes,
a blue halo flashing on his head,

keen as the wind streaming over the roofs,
herding the traffic aside.

Night Run, Mount Merrion, 1975
for Dom

That impulse — to strip and sprint —
past crowds, across a football pitch, a screen —
would have blown past like any season
of yellowed newsprint

if you hadn't caught in it a flash
of your own impulse, to throw night airs
on our friendship: lit window-squares
on a wooded suburban hill marking our dash

and not one twitching curtain, no one to see
our unrehearsed *Midsummer*: intimate
earth with a different spin on it,
our bodies gone to our heads —

cool grass, twigs, footlights of the city spread
livid, streaking through trees.

Roundstone
i.m. Barbara Nolan

Our best times together we were always on holiday
from ourselves. I heard you kept
something of your insouciance; in your last weeks

throwing a party at your house in the Allihies,
laughing as you told a friend how strange it was
to know you were dying and not

believe it. Remember our first play
at being lovers — a cottage with a loft bed
in the breathing thatch, the broad hearth
big enough for a child to stand in.

We'd stoop under the mantle into that
uncovered well-space framing
an airy rectangle of stars,

our faces lit by the clarity, rising towards it.

A Brief History Of Snowflakes

'Every snowflake that falls to earth has its own unique history'
— John Hallett, *New Scientist*, 2013

Conception isn't as easy as it might seem:
chancy, incremental, no sudden sprawl
into symmetry. Each begins on high:
a cold droplet meeting a speck
of pollen or dust, a weld
between earth and sky

after which things fall
into predetermined spaces
as molecules move into crystals,
glitter-fractals of silence, loosening
the world's graininess, out of which is spun
this finishing touch that melts on your tongue.

Collector's Items

i.m. Jim Morrison

Matchboxes, epitaphs, butterflies
and murmurations, tornadoes,
vintage pinups, glass eyes —
or there are those
who veer off into some zone
far from the zoo,
something entirely their own,

like the artist I knew
who'd served in the territorials
and arranged — on a shelf high
above his bed — plastic dolls
naked and unwashed, wild
hair stiffened with mud;
an antediluvian family
salvaged from the flood,

preserved forensically,
as they'd been found,
wearing only the war paint
of the abandoned —
equipped, ready to haunt
or follow my friend
whose heart went
years before I remembered
to ask him what they meant.

Beds

Going to bed, we closed
the clattery old shutters, and woke
trampled by the child bouncing
to unbolt the morning.

*

Auden's face was less
'a wedding cake left out in the rain'
than a rumpled bed, slept-
and loved-in.

*

What's under yours? Suitcases, shoes,
the dust-drift, the trapdoor, the chute
that drops you into that gulf
where the mind has you, all to itself.

*

The night after my mother died
blankets were no use: roof and walls
blown away, interstellar winds
entered from all sides.

*

Rembrandt slept in a half-bed. To lie horizontal
would be to invite
the vertical, gold-leafed night
to fall.

*

What it comes to:
pillow-silence, a lover's tangled hair —
face of her uncombed dreams —
turned to you.

Nativity

No one believes in you:
formidable seed

wriggling blindly
to unlock

the terrible accident
that made you

a big book — doorstopper
riding within

your mother's risen skin —
dropped somewhere

under a lucky or
unlucky star, the edge

of an always empire
spreading like lichen on

our planet's rim — No,
everyone takes

a fought-over fragment
of the tale, valuable

as a holy bone robed
in marble and plutonium:

a story washed clean
of its afterbirth and

the reasons we raise
our voices in a vaulted room

whose ideal light is
dim, bandaged and stained.

Marvellous

Another filthy night in a week of gales,
our big sash-windows rattling so hard
I had to wedge bits of cardboard between their frames.
The doorbell might have been going for some time
before I noticed.
                I thought it must be my aunt
come down from her upstairs flat to look in on my mother.

A stranger stood there,
                a man in a yellow anorak,
wet hair flat on his skull, clutching in his left hand
a paper bag, his face bearded and solemn,
the eyes meeting mine head-on (or staring through me),
the voice clear, urgent:
                'You think you're marvellous
you think you're marvellous you think you're marvellous...'

Monotonous but with feeling, a needle dropped
in the midst of a record, skipping, repeating, scratching
my lame response:
                'I'm sorry but I think you have the wrong ...'
'You think you're marvellous you think you're marvellous
you think you're marvellous — This is for you.'

He was holding towards me the crumpled paper bag
that might have contained a half-finished takeaway meal
or a bunch of severed fingers. His other hand
was in his anorak pocket, gripping something
dangerous? Hardly, but still,
                on his locked stare
I closed the door. Standing in the narrow hall,
I heard the theme tune: my mother settling in
for *Coronation Street*.
                Along our rain-lashed avenue,
a fellow human was on the loose, somewhat lost,
perhaps wandering house to house with his paper bag
and scrap of a message: a torch with a faltering battery,
a missed connection sparking into the future,

becoming something else:
                        our rickety old flat
in that period house, decades before we left,
my mother alive with her arthritis, our cat Claire
asleep on the boxy TV; me standing there
as if I had just stepped in, having travelled miles
through the corrosive dark —
                      This is for you.

'There Is No Loitering Permitted Till 7 a.m.'

My first taste of La Nausée:
I was nineteen, up late
in grandmother's drawing room

when I saw — really *saw* — my hand
under the lamp: these naked
blunt peninsulas where

all my creaturliness stopped.
My hand was that of a species,
a *thing* that was also a *me* —

and I had to be up and away,
closing the front door quietly,
walking rapidly, as if

I had somewhere to get to,
passing through sleeping suburbs
putting the hours and miles

behind me. On Baggot Street Bridge,
I leant on the wall, to allow
light on the Grand Canal

dawn on my exhausted brain,
not noticing the Guard
till he had materialised

beside me. He took out a notebook
and demanded my name, and where
I was coming from (*Officer,*

where do I start?)

Newts

Water boatmen skimmed and darted, reeds stood
in coppery pools. Above us, dragonflies
stop-framed, printing their iridescence.

It was enough to know the difference
between a frog and that olive-grey
sliver with a sunrise on its belly. Was it
a fortnight or just one solitary

afternoon panelled in yellow-blue air?
I was ten and a half, my cousins
eight, six and four. Nobody called us
and we never caught any newts. I open this door

to remember how it feels to be poured
outside time, into the fall of a moment
fulfilling itself without any need to know it.

Torremolinos, 1972

Maybe when he saw me standing outside the record shop
in the white-hot siesta
he thought I was older than fifteen
(though I probably looked younger.)

Maybe when he said 'I like your hat'
(a camel-skin cowboy hat my mother had bought me
in Tangiers), his appraisal was in another language
he thought I might have known.

Maybe he didn't see how flattered I was,
to be complimented, casually,
by a man twice my age.

Maybe, when he asked if I'd like to go for a drink,
he didn't guess I assumed he meant a glass of Coke
in some nearby streetside café.

Maybe he had no idea
how impossible it would have been for me
to run away (like demanding to be let off a plane)
when he turned into a side street, then
unlocked the door to a house.

Maybe when he shot the bolt and drew the blinds
he was oblivious to the shock
that went through me: my certainty
I had sleepwalked into some terrible dream
too unreal to wake from.

Maybe he would have been startled by the images
strobing behind my eyes: nothing sexual,
but torture, dismemberment: panels from my favourite
horror comics, *Creepy* and *Eerie*.

Maybe it was this weird naivety
that protected me.

Maybe when I said 'Please,
can I go now?', it was a strain
of kindness moved him to smile,
gently part the hair on my forehead,
and unbolt the door.

Pinball Wizard

At sixteen, I was on top
of the world, prising loose
big wedges of scree,

to watch them wobble
like liberated wheels
down a hill in West Cork,

fascinated as each sliver
of landslide gathered momentum,
to topple and finally die

in a far field. The last one,
almost as big as a boulder,
rumbled in a kind of slow

motion, bounced and crashed
over bigger rocks, ripped through
heather, gorse and a grove

of saplings, unstoppable,
slicing a diagonal line
across bright bracken, till all

that barricaded my missile —
from the whitewashed gable
of a cottage I had managed to not
see —

was a low, drystone wall
that half-collapsed but held,
and it hit me.

'Alright, Full Auto'

> — *the last recorded words of Charles Vacca,*
> *instructor at Bullets & Burgers, Las Vegas*

So this army vet allows a skinny
nine-year-old girl full control of an Uzi,

sleepwalking under that bizarre
Voodoo: the right to bear

magic wands that really work,
or because — as the owner

Sam Scarmardo said in an interview —
'...this was big, something high

on her bucket list to do.'

Gastarbeiter

In Munich in 1979, a rumour:
vacancies in the city morgue for washers of corpses.
The money, apparently, was good.

How difficult could it be?
Could I have the stomach for it?

Be able, that is, to ablute, sponge
the bloated or skeletal-old,
mashed, mangled, dismembered

or, perhaps worse, the barely blemished:
the old man who was the spit of —
the runaway with the snake tattoo she never told —

a place (as I imagined it) broad
as a warehouse, strip-lit, a sour

fluorescence, flickering now
on me, working a sponge — stopped
by a sniffle of wind in the ducts, a settling sheet —

something barely more than this
released breath, as I straighten up, weirdly vertical.

Customs

for Molly & Adrian

Where I come from
buildings are circular
because The Devil conceals Himself
in corners.

Where I come from
talking to oneself
is a certified sign of sanity.

Where I come from,
when the moon is full,
we leave out a saucer of milk
in case the moon people are thirsty.

Where I come from
we prefer to point
with our lips.

Where I come from
we set aside a day
to unbury the dead,
hold them above our heads,
and dance.

1: Rural US (specifically barns). 2 & 3: Seems reasonable.
4: Nicaragua. 5: Madagascar.

Wild Garlic

Bitter as wild garlic: a Donegal curse.
Food of tin miners, famine foragers... so rank
it found its way into the ink
marking boundaries on old maps. Search

and you'll find such fragments, a flavour
of hunger, a working spell laid
along the riverbank; in the wooded shade
a ruffling, matt-green floor,

each tapering leaf an exhalation
tickling the air. It seems you crossed
some kind of boundary, trespassed
on a carpeted underworld, an exhumation

whose bare feet follow as you emerge
into the cloud-light, loosely covered in earth.

The Air, The Aether

seemed thicker then.
Dusk was a weaver's loom
of numinous flitterings.
Disbelief made no sense
when weighty things
clambered down the dependable
rungs of the ladder: succubi
with enough flesh on their bones
to empty your lungs.

One day, surely, we'd learn
how not to ruffle the lie
of what we trod and what
swilled in us, below high
cut-glass configurations —
humours, tides, balances,
black bile, yellow bile,
surfaces you could disturb
and be disturbed by —

From The East

So much sifting
of cloud
into cold
fine flour.

So swift
this overnight shift
into drifts.

Such thickening,
every car
a blanched
boulder.

Such foundering,
each footstep
unable to sound
the road's
submarine
dream.

Such a load
off the air's
shoulders

and such a press
against doors
and glass
and my eyelids

of something like
speechlessness
fully dressed.

In The Name Of

the blue tip
night-splitter
dew-beater
flimshift
creak-of-first-light

rise for us.

In the name of

the song-scatterer
overrim
day-tilt
hemlift
star-thinner

all rise.

Just Now

voices climb and are blown
in from the street,
the dog is asleep
with one ear
lifted and alert
as sunlight lengthens
the hairline crack that is
a daddy-longlegs' shadow.

Song Between Seasons
after Flann O'Brien

Winter breathes
on the pane;
no, we're back
in Spring again,

nothing nips
at our fingers,
gloves come off,
warm air lingers —

curling leaves
hesitate;
seasons miss
their sell-by date,

read the signs
or carry on,
uncertain times,
uncertain song —

Westport, Late August

for Seán Lysaght

Streets are buttressed with windshields
screening the sky's blue gaps
curdled with grey. We are idling

over coffee, as if we had all day,
which we do, sitting in the thick
of the bustle and flow: a cool

bristle of rain ('a smirr' you say)
followed by a sober-suited
funeral — slow bells, a flavour

of something, someone, that calls
for making a momentary
diversion — You mention

the swallows you've seen, late
as October — 'They must live
in some archway near here... and then

one day you notice they're gone' —

Two Street Portraits

GIRL WITH PYTHON, VANCOUVER

She is sitting on the warm pavement,
in a crop top and shades,

the snake's thick, kinked coils —
a sepia-black archipelago —

hooked loosely on her tanned neck,
the head's blunt arrow

resting on her bare shoulder;
both of them seeming content,

a picture of apparently calm
entanglement.

READING ROOM

At a bend in the rush hour — where Leinster Street
swerves into Lincoln Place —
the lanky, bearded man in the baseball cap
is settled in a niche of the red-bricked
Dental Hospital — that was Finn's Hotel
in another life, another book. Here,
he reads, paperbacks and newspapers; marginal yet
integral, folded into a space
so thoroughly his own, I always look for him:
absorbed, paper cup set
beside him on the pavement's armrest, like
an afterthought (which perhaps it is.)

Accosted

I'm twenty-five, walking on the sunny side of a street
in San Francisco — probably Church or Cole —

when I am visited by an awareness keen
as the warmth on my face and arms,

as if things have finally slipped into place, my life
clothed in a new skin — bright

as the absurdly yellow Victorian house,
our bedroom with the bay window —

though nothing's in place, I'm coasting,
my girlfriend already tired of my indolent dreaminess.

Happiness: it clasps your arm, stops you
in the street, then lets you go —

Workshop

Find your personal lexicon, your best
and precious word-hoard. Make a list
of favourites — *hoard, lexicon, spindrift, drought,
saccade, arabesque, smithereens* — the kind your mouth
was shaped for: *socket, vermilion, pilfer, dross* —

Now think of the sort of characters you'd cross
the road to avoid, ones you'd curse with a grim
vocabulary — *relatable, loser, 'going
forward', mansplaining, Sad!* — and cheerful tips
like *wake-up-and-smell-the... read my...* Close their lips

till they swallow your medicine, this nourishing
they were born to spit out, sing.

On Difficulty

If its passage leaves a hum in the rails,
a twist of dust on the road,
that's enough. I don't mind
if it travels ahead of me
(I'm slow. I read with my ears.)
so long as there is a sense
of sinewy music. My difficulty
with difficulty is when I suspect
the accident is staged, and if
I called in the whole crew
to meticulously unpick the pile-up,
removing wreck after wreck,
I'd find nothing to rescue
but a clutch of crash-test dummies.

Footnotes For Ovid

> *Let the day come that rounds off*
> *my uncertain span. The work is done.*
> — Metamorphosis: Envoi

> *At the same time, [...] the Empire was flooded with ecstatic cults. For all its Augustan stability, it was at sea in hysteria and despair, at one extreme wallowing in the bottomless appetites and suffering of the gladiatorial arena, and at the other searching higher and higher for a spiritual transcendence — which eventually did take form, on the crucifix.*
> — Ted Hughes, introduction to 'Tales From Ovid', 1997

1.

Begin, again, at the start: how a shower spills
black coins on a warm pavement — smells
of earth's dust rousing and running, beginning to stir
the prow of an olive leaf in a Roman gutter.

2.

While the old world slept on the brink of a new star sign,
you orchestrated your song of bodies changed —
clambering, tripping on shadows — into new forms;

incestuous tangle of gods and humans deranged
by passions, bodies and minds a disturbed swarm;
energies dark as the Primal Chaos, galaxies

galloping apart, Earth's blood (a warm embrace
broken for good — how everything in time flees
from itself, for another body, another place,

forsaking its lucky day in the sun to flick
the channel: another spark for the old theme
that is always new as The Odyssey, your lineage, fit

to carry us to the end of the Anthropocene.

3.

Exiled for *carmen et error*, whatever the mistake,
you had the last word, *vivam*. Your song escaped,
resurfacing like those dolphins you saw, each lucent,
embodied wave your freewheeling testament.

4.

Call it the Age of Would-Be Giants, days
of nostalgia for 'greatness', 'the people', 'strong' men
chanted into power, as blind to omen
as the weakest emperors, given to Midas-displays —
gold-fevered bathroom fittings, penthouses, lifts —
unable to form one classic thought or settle
longer than it takes to hurl a mountain or piss
that no-longer-precious metal.

5.

Beards whiten. Hair, when shaken, tinkles
with tiny icicles.

The rest of the body cowers as the polar Boreas
whistles and blows The Black Sea into glass.

Walking out onto that slippery roof,
you gauge its solidity, uncracked even by hooves;

looking towards the horizon, note
the absence of dolphins, an ice-anchored boat,

and, below your feet, the fish pent
in windowed cells, some of them breathing yet.

Latinate

HADRIAN'S FAREWELL

Sad, soul,
to see you, whose laughter
was part of my furniture,
turned out of your bolthole —

ODI, AMO

I hate, I love: harmonics in a ruin,
all I'm in tune with being out of tune.

From The Irish:
Three Triads & Two Fragments

THREE TRIADS

Three who won't see sense:
A prince riding to war.
A Viking wading ashore.
A moron millions adore.

Three murderers of desire:
The fear of a jealous spouse.
The finding of a louse.
An intruder in the house.

Three narrow things that support us:
The milk-stream from the cow's udder.
The narrowness of the natal door.
The slenderness of being here.

from PIARAS FEIRITÉAR'S LAMENT
FOR THE DEATH IN FLANDERS
OF MUIRIS MAC GEARAILT

In Dingle the wailing blew in with the sea wind
louder and shriller, and the merchants huddled
and grew afraid. They needn't have worried.
Banshees do not lament their kind.

MEETING ON THE ROAD TO SWORDS

'Good day, scholar. Where are you from?'
'Clonmacnoise. My learning is done.'
'How are things there?' 'Perfectly fine,
foxes gnaw at the Abbot's spine.'

Pangur Dubh

— *after Pangur Bán, Anon, 9th century*

I make this prayer to God above
to help our poor cat, Pangur Dubh.
It must be seven months ago
he caught a mouse, then let it go.

From lauds to vespers, days are long
and all monks here arise at dawn,
and each of us must play his part:
to farm and pray and ply this art

that colours every word I spell
like water drawn from a well,
while this cat drowses, half-asleep.
Can he be moved to earn his keep

and get a thrill (like his white twin)
in wars that only cats can win,
impaling mice on those sharp claws,
obeying Nature's simple laws?

Or are they simple? Who can find
the trapdoor to this creature's mind,
inscrutable as any text
that has me up, past midnight, vexed,

distracted by the mice that run
through library and scriptorium,
while Pangur sleeps on, fathomless,
a pool of darkness near my desk.

But when he stirs and, yawning, wakes
and stretches with that feline grace,
in bestiaries of cats and mice,
his mere existence will suffice.

Silk
for Trish

My first serious girlfriend walked stately
in faded pyjama trousers, their cuffs
cinched with yellow and green silk ribbons
under a kind of petticoat, a complication
of skirts and blouses: a pigtail, heady wafts
of patchouli — anything she touched
exhaled it forever.
                        She had a real job
with an ad agency. One of her friends
was a tall, handsome, bearded tramp
who carried a staff like Moses and strode
purposefully and endlessly.
                              We were,
if not paired, a pair. A hash-smoking, green-eyed
middleclass Mount Merrion peasant, and me
in army cast-offs, speaking through hair
I could sit on. It seemed we were twinned
worry-beads, perfectly matched. I
was smitten, utterly.
                          On the threshold
of lovership, she hesitated (not
so much as a kiss or hug or hand-
hold) for eleven precocious months, till
I met her in Tobin's to walk out.
                                    She called
eight years later, back home briefly
from barge-life in Amsterdam, and we sat
in a warm crowded afternoon, on bar stools
in Grogan's, both of us out of fancy dress;
she in a blue and white tartan shirt, me
with my haystack sheared off for good.
                                        It must have been
the 80s, nearly four decades ago. Odd
to recall so clearly the way our pleasant talk skirted
and circled, and the Dublin poet who broke in

to bum a pint and a tenner.
                                        So, the little roads
tangle and twine, turn
from crossroads to roundabouts to something
that overlaps — untouching — ripples and
lifts, easily as silk.

Pub
— London, 1989

Somewhere along the Walworth Road
we stepped out of the sunny day.
At the back, chairs had been cleared.
A rock anthem clubbed at the walls.

Small and wiry, she was already
down to a gold lamé bikini.
A few punters whooped and cheered.
Others were silent, perhaps troubled

by that look: a fixed grimace
of unutterable contempt, carried
with what seemed a practiced skill,
like a trayful of foaming glasses

she must never spill.

Crossing Hungerford Bridge

you said look down, and I saw them,
a scatter of old skateboards
on a concrete island, one of the bridge supports.

Thrown there, it seemed, to lie
exhausted, like a patina of wet leaves,
below this windy walkway rocked
by criss-crossing trains, drowning a busker's guitar.

A game maybe, or something more sombre:
a fallen clatter of wings, a salvaging
laid like wreaths, riding the dark water

in memory of who or what,
other than those
who stepped into their South Bank souls
surfing the roaring concrete beneath their feet.

Three Towers
— *Pieter Bruegel The Elder*

THE GREAT TOWER

A fine, hazy day for it, nothing but a skelf
of steam-coloured cloud clinging to an upper tier.

Fort, coliseum, arch upon reinforced arch,
it gyres above the townland at its base,

into a high-rise ruin, monument
to a world where everyone drones in the same tongue.

On a hill in the foreground, masons bow before
the pointed boot of King Nimrod. Detail is all:

a galleon approaching the busy quay has a sailor
climbing the rigging; two stories up, inside

the wheel of a treadmill crane, two men tread
eternally forwards. Heaven is a matter of time

spiralling into a pristine sky, and only a bird
likely to fly into it.

THE LITTLE TOWER

Something has tightened. Nimrod is gone, with the masons
and most of the hill in the foreground, and the town
has reverted to fields. The harbour is still there,
galleons and smaller craft busy as water flies.

Though the painting is half a size smaller, the tower
is taller and more complete. It is still a raw hive
open to weather, and the clouds it pierces are darker
and more substantial, a grey-green armada.

Look closer and it's like lifting a stone to peer
at a teeming metropolis almost too small for the eye:
labourers, dockhands... lost in the inner distance

of craft, bright clink of iron on stone, the plumb line
dangling, the helix turned, the roof being raised
out of the picture, out of his working hands.

THE LOST TOWER

A miniature, painted on ivory, it is listed once
in the inventory of the famous miniaturist
Guilio Clovio. It may have been commissioned
by the merchant banker Nicolaes Jonghlinck.
The emperor Rudolph II may have added it
to his collection of Bruegels. But there are no
further records. Nobody knows for certain

whose intent gaze it was reflected in:
a miniature of a miniature; or who mislaid it,
forgot to include it in a will, destroyed or
abandoned it to the bottom drawer
of a razed house, a missing part
(of an animal of biblical proportions) — no less
luminous for being lost.

The Verdict On Chagall

'...green, purple and red Jews shooting out of the earth,
fiddling on violins, flying through the air...'
In the words of the new German authorities, you can hear
an attempt to scribble over this 'assault' on poor
'Western Civilisation', as if it were the victim
that must barricade itself from time to time
in panicky walls, lest it become submerged

in buoyant, aquatic light — greens, purples, reds —
moons afloat with flowers and fiddlers, lovers and cows,
villages with yellow rooms you can swim through,
surfacing without breaking the surface, if only you step
out of these bloodied and soiled clothes, into your first
skin, the one that never learned how to be
terrified by a lack of gravity.

Deansgrange Similes

Like my mother's gravity and drift
so many years after her last
rainfall of roses and dirt;

like the others time-leased in this
undulant stone wave;
like the singular trees

(in particular that warped birch
swaying in a sudden cold shower,
trailing its skirts

in time with the shaggy old cypress
framed in the arched window
of her last address);

like the visitors observing dates
on private calendars; like the words
and the lost for words: the late

departed, remembered, prayed for,
dearly beloved, missed,
survived by, always, forever;

like the suburb's expanded brawl
of busyness (the old cottages
opposite the cemetery wall

endlessly buffeted
by lorries on the main road,
their window-frames flushed

with evening sun); like the occasion
and the mind's inadequacy,
its attraction

to elliptical orbits, fled
and ever-fixed, adrift
with our space-faring dead.
   Deansgrange Cemetery, Dublin, 2020

Two Endings
i.m. Anthony Glavin

It's been playing in my head all morning:
last night's dream, in which I am spending time
with Anthony, my older friend and mentor;
talking about nothing serious, neither of us
rubbing the other up the wrong way.

I don't often meet Anthony in dreams,
though his presence is always to hand: humorous, stern,
standing behind me, ready to hijack the mouse
and hit delete, like the time he handed back
my first MS, divided into two
A4 envelopes, the slimmest one titled
Possibly, With More Work and the other,
twice as thick, *Flogging A Dead Horse*.

He was someone you could call in the small hours
to hear that steadying voice: 'It's alright,
it's only a panic attack; you're not going to die.'

When emphysema imprisoned him, I carried a pager
for emergencies, worries, frettings:
on my second date with the woman I'd marry,
apologising for abandoning her in the cinema
as the lights dimmed for *The Man Who Wasn't There*.

I wasn't, the night he died in The Mater,
six months after his heart-lung transplant.
I'd witnessed the post-op surge of possibility —
his voice returned, his hope for three more years,
enough time to finish his long poem, travel to India —
then the rapid slide, his exhausted, brittle body
rejecting the organs, his voice gone for good.

I hadn't seen him in weeks and wasn't prepared
for his appearance: huddled in a low-lit room,
unmoving, a big tube in his side.

Did I say something lame? Did I even speak?
He shot me one withering glance and turned to the wall.
And that was it. Nothing can dream away
or disremember that look. I can only displace it

with an afternoon, years earlier, in St Michael's,
when they had to put him back on the ventilator.
'I'll be right here', he said, pressing my forehead,
quoting ET: his light touch, commonplace, real
as sunlight on a stripped bed, that indelible smile.

Bodily

THE DAY AFTER

at work, grinning, she said: 'I often
used to look at your crotch.'
So I confessed
I had often looked at her breasts.

DREAM

'How's your night going', I asked
the broadly-smiling barmaid
and woke with a taste, a crumb
of chocolate cherry lipstick
melting on my tongue.

STEPLADDER

She asked me to hold it steady.
As she unscrewed the light bulb, her jumper
rode up and revealed part of her belly,
which was one of the reasons I
asked if she's doing anything, later.

NAUTICAL

Unhooking her bra, I whispered: 'It creaks
like a ship's rigging', and she
laughed: 'Now *that's* poetry.'

BATHING PLACE

At seventy-one, she's delighted to discover
an unembarrassed carnality: 'Fellas your age
have to be careful, keep their gaze
to themselves, but if *I* want to stare
at that young man, I will. Nobody owns the air.'

Colonoscopy

What else should I write, arriving in the lounge
of late middle age? File this: magnesium citrate,
sweetened with aspartame, sounds like how it tastes.

'Date of birth?' 'Are you on any medications?'
A crisp young intern ticks each box, rips off
the BP cuff, and is gone in a puff of soap.

Plenty of time to think about friends I know
who've been looked into. The same breezy corridor
from delivery room to where bad dreams transpire.

Soon now, good-humoured Mr Maguire
will redo the clumsy catheter, titrate the slow
milligrams of midazolam, and I'll be

a map of the city, a tube train running through
the softest of soft tissue: what x-rays show
as loops and folds, a pillowcase of smoke.

Post Op

And just like that, a small
enigmatic part removed, leaving me,
if anything, at a further remove.

Above the hospital golf course
and expensive south-Dublin roofs
(smothered, it seems, in trees),

I have the luxury
of being eye to eye
with the soft-headed mountains.

On the TV, Gaza
is being flattened: hospitals, schools...
smeared into ashy blurs,

and look, six floors below,
one tiny figure — a man's —
is towing his golf cart

onto the pool-table green,
slightly stooped, as if he bears
the entire weightlessness of the world.

Mixture

Rummaging in a kitchen drawer,
I find an old electricity bill
with a recipe written in green marker
in my wife's neat writing.

The first three lines are clear:

1 tbsp melted butter
1 egg yolk
¼ tsp vanilla

A splash of water has dissolved
much of the rest of it
into a Greenland-shaped blot.

Picking it up, I can make out:

1 ½ — own sugar
½ —
— powder
— choc chips

and something I'd missed:
next to the egg yolk,
in much smaller letters,
our teenage son's contribution,
underlined:
       SOME DEATH
                and
(perhaps to dilute that)

a little green heart.

Mark

is my first mark, a brand
sealed
with a dabbing hand:

what I became
and part
of what

I assume
will one day be read
by the rain.

The way a name
is an ark
that can contain — head
to toe —

a person
(Eve, Aram,
Cleo
or Cain),

is a kind of magic,
the human kind — more
smoke than
mirror.

I rise
stretching each day
pulling the M
over
my head, pushing

my feet
into the tangled
trouser-legs
of the K.

I am a Mark.
Who
(meaning what mark)
are you?

Crown Shyness

> *...a phenomenon observed in some tree species,*
> *in which the crowns of fully stocked trees*
> *do not touch each other, forming channel-like gaps.*
>
> — Wikipedia

If you want to see the pattern that they've made
you need to look up from the forest floor
in summer. Ends of branches don't abrade

each other, but leave ripples in their shade,
as if they've grown wary of that war
that moves inside the pattern that they've made.

Mapping the movements of the winds that flayed
and thrashed their heads till they became heart sore,
they made room for whatever might abrade.

It took time. Now the channels are inlaid
and every shivering tip has taken score,
moving in time with the pattern that they've made.

Seams in the brainy dark, a bright cascade,
a shyness almost human at its core,
a canopy of gaps that can't abrade;

no matter how many arguments have swayed
the trees, the wood — the gap between the door
and frame describes the pattern we have made,
that only stillness and silence will abrade.

Understory

for Michael

I lie back. All it takes
to visit some wooded place

is for me to remember your
story: half-brother I never

imagined till mum gave me
a bundle of letters you'd sent

she never knew how to answer.
Her first-born: adopted child

of an Irish soldier; brought up
in a house on a Brighton hilltop,

a garden dandering off
into fields crowned with a wood

that drew you into your first
adventure: a bright meadow,

cow parsley nodding and buzzing
above you: the child

entering the taller tale
that may or may not shelter you

from the blue-grey storm cloud
darkening the nearby downs:

all of which raises inside you
a bubble of song — 'something

religious, a hymn, but nothing
to do with that...' — sown

in a wildwood suburb, a voice
reaching in the cow parsley

an altitude all its own.

Everything You Always Wanted To Know

At fifteen, I found Burt Reynolds in my mother's bed,
stowed under her pillow in a Cosmo centrefold.

Impossibly hairy, recumbent on a bearskin rug,
a chewed cigarillo between his lips —

He was grinning, happy to be discovered,
even as I slid him back

where I'd found him; like the miraculous medal
she'd hidden under my mattress,

like the legion of things that can never
be spoken; and what would remain unsaid

about the convent girl who'd strayed
enough to give birth to two children; how she found

ways to widen a single bed, and kick
her cold, Catholic hot water bottle onto the floor.

The Themes

How many times can I praise
sunlight on water, on stone,
tiny or great absences and
the modest elbow room a poem
makes for itself? Sometimes
I wonder if I fell into the wrong
preoccupation, being more
daydreamer than thinker,
a tinkerer of thoughts
slipping their own knots,
a boy halfway up the stairs,
stopped by an odd cloud
in the landing window,
who has long since forgotten
what he was going down for.

20-1-18

A postcard arrived today, from aunt Moira (dead
since 2010) to my mother, who'd followed her
not long after. No postmark. It must have been
delayed for a decade at least, since Moira,
who spent her last few years in a nursing home,
is up and about on a holiday in Cornwall
(a forgettable shot of picturesque fishing boats
moored below a mock-Tudor pub: The Chain Link.)
Maybe it slept in that hollow, 'the dead letter place',
till someone unearthed it. The message is what we'd expect,
warm-blooded phrases never designed for more
than love's housekeeping work, its breakfast table:
Dear Sheila, I'm here in Penzance with Paul.
The scenery is out of this world...

The End, Etc.

The world ended on October 22, 1844,
as William Miller's disciple had predicted it would.

We are living in its aftermath, along with all those
descendants of the Millerites who came through
what became known as The Great Disappointment,

to regroup as The Adventists, then
The Seventh Day Adventists, who now
have a worldwide membership of 20 million souls.

The human mind is a stepped-on ant
that miraculously unsquishes itself, to invent
Braille, write *A Brief History of Time*

or reinforce an old material, so it may prove
impervious to the slightest trickle of doubt
or the weight of a toddler's sandal, which is

the weight of the world insufferably carrying on.

Checkout
— for all workers on the front line of indifference

Too often irritated by ones
who have time for a few friendly words,
I was caught off-guard when she
answered my innocuous 'How'ye'
with 'I'm well, and how are *you*?'

When she responded to my 'Can't
complain' with 'That's good, isn't it?'
(and I answered with words of less
substance than the breath
that launched them), she told me

that in the last two years
twelve people she'd loved had died.
When I said 'That's terrible', she smiled:
'Yes, but they're here now,
standing around us as we speak.'

One of them was her best friend.
'She always had a great sense
of humour, that one, always saying,
"will you ever get over yourself?
Honestly, will you ever..."

All this as if the talk
were not touched by anything
other than the patter that halts
unscanned items; as if I
were not touched in my turn.

If there were others in the queue
shuffling, curling their toes
(as I too often had been),
I was unaware of them, paused
in the doorway of a checkout parlour,

a guest among the shades.

Ah, Jesus

what is it about your name
and the taking of it, that yet-to-be-tapped-out vein —

the way we fondle it
like a wedding ring in a pocket —

the way you star in a song, put a kick
in a joke or a story: 'What Furniture Would Jesus Pick?' —

the way you find yourself nailed in so many tats
on so many murderers' backs —

the way, when we curse or cum,
those sibilants are Braille for the blind tongue —

the way you are still the flayed talisman, last cry
of the fallen, if also the fall guy —

the way your dashboard afterlife is set
against the roll of the road, our last wild bet —

Road

as itself, gritted, tarred, cambered just enough to shake off the rain —

as Ferris wheel of landscape and cloud —

as the median grass strip tickling the car's belly —

as wakefulness, wiper-thump, rain's metronome —

as divining rod for evening, dawn, the poured tar of the night —

as head-beams stoking a corner, a stage-lit fox —

as the short cut that isn't —

as indigo mountains, partings in woods, bright shrine of a forecourt —

as layers of heat-shimmer, makings of a mirage —

as uplift and grief, with the world under its heel —

as caravan, convoy, baggage carousel of the refugee —

as the longest long acre —

as milestones that clock you: the derelict farmhouse, all eyes —

as the hitchhiker's dice —

as *Where the hell is this?* —

as return to the hinterland, the one sure-fire road —

as world tightening to a lane, a drive where you pull up the road's ladder —

as whatever you're having and one more for itself —

Notes

Regarding the poems from the Latin and Irish, these are not translations, but versions, departures or what Derek Mahon might have called adaptations.

Page 53:   Footnotes For Ovid
The final section refashions some images and observations from a prose translation of a poem by Ovid, 'Exile By The Black Sea', in *The Penguin Book of Latin Verse* (1962), edited and translated by Frederick Brittain.

Page 55:   Latinate
As with the last poem in the Ovid sequence, I adapted Hadrian's Farewell from a prose translation in *The Penguin Book of Latin Verse* (1962), edited and translated by Frederick Brittain.

Page 56:   From The Irish: Three Triads And Two Fragments
The three triads are from cribs by Frank O'Connor and Kuno Meyer. O'Connor described the triad as 'the simplest of all mnemonics', developed 'before the Irish learned to read or write', later used as literary exercises by 'students in native schools.' I have altered and refashioned two of these in a more contemporary idiom.

The first quatrain is from a considerably longer lament by Piaras Feiritéar. I adapted it from part of a 1932 translation by Ua Duinnín, quoted in Patricia Lysaght's book-length study, *The Banshee* ((The O'Brien Press, 1996):

> In Dingle the crying did not grow faint,
> And the hoarding merchants grew afraid,
> But they need not fear for themselves,
> Banshees do not bewail their sort.

The original Irish is also given in the introduction:

> Ins an Daingean níor chaigil an cheol-ghol,
> Gur ghlac eagla ceannaidhthe an chnósta,
> Dá n-eagla féin níor bhaoghal dóibh sin,
> Ní chaoinid mná sidhe an sórt soin.

The second quatrain is from what Frank O'Connor describes as 'a bitter little fragment', probably 11th century. As with the triads, I have altered and refashioned images and rhymes, etc.

Page 57:   Pangur Dubh
Pangur Dubh (Black Pangur) is a response to the anonymous 9th century poem, Pangur Bán (White Pangur), written by a monk about his pet cat. The original poem has been translated several times, by Robin Flower, Seamus Heaney and Paul Muldoon, among others.

Page 75:   Everything You Always Wanted To Know
The sex manual by Californian psychiatrist David Reuben, *Everything You Always Wanted To Know About Sex* (*But Were Afraid To Ask)*, was published in 1969. Woody Allen's film of the same title, in which Burt Reynolds had a cameo role, was released in 1972.

Acknowledgments

Acknowledgments are due to the print and online publications where a number of the following poems first appeared: *The Irish Times, The New Statesman, The Friday Poem, Poetry Ireland Review, The Café Review, The High Window, Trasna, Trumpet, Crannóg, Cyphers, The Honest Ulsterman, Anthropocene, The North, Magma.*

Some of these poems appeared in the following anthologies: *Metamorphic: 21st Century Poets Respond To Ovid* (edited by Nessa O'Mahony and Paul Munden, Recent Work Press, 2017), *Ten Poems About Getting Older* (selected and introduced by John McCullough, Candlestick Press, 2021), *Local Wonders* (edited by Pat Boran, Dedalus Press, 2021), *Romance Options: Love Poems For Today* (edited by Leeanne Quinn and Joseph Woods, Dedalus Press, 2022).

The poem 'Checkout' was selected by Carol Ann Duffy for her online anthology of pandemic poems, *Write Where We Are Now* (Manchester University, 2020), and the poem 'Wild Garlic' was included in the 2023 Poetry Jukebox/Quotidian curation for *Forage*, selected by Maria McManus and Emma Must.

Special thanks to Seán Lysaght, Mark Roper and Christian Stevens for their close readings and invaluable suggestions; to Patrick Mac Allister and David Stephenson for their feedback and encouragement, and to Allister and Carol Anne O'Brien for relaying a fragment of family history that gave me the little poem, 'Civil'.

I am immensely grateful to An Chomhairle Ealaíon/The Arts Council for a Covid Response Award in 2020 and a Literature Bursary in 2021.

MARK GRANIER is a writer and photographer based in Bray, Co Wicklow. His previous collections are *Ghostlight: New & Selected Poems* (Salmon, 2017), *Haunt* (Salmon, 2015), *Fade Street* (Salt, 2010), *The Sky Road* (Salmon, 2007) and *Airborne* (Salmon, 2001). Prizes include The Vincent Buckley Poetry Prize and two Patrick and Katherine Kavanagh Poetry Fellowships.

salmonpoetry
Cliffs of Moher, County Clare, Ireland

"Publishing the finest Irish and international literature."
Michael D. Higgins, President of Ireland